Gardening WITH THE EXPERTS

PRUNING

Gardening WITH THE EXPERTS

PRUNING

Moira Ryan

HARLAXTON
PUBLISHING

Photographs: Douglass Baglin Photography courtesy Weldon Trannies: page 44.
Bay Picture Library: pages 7, 15, 38 (below), 42 (left).
Mary Moody: pages 8, 9, 20 (below).
Manuel Patty: pages 17, 26.
Pamela Polglase: pages 14, 22-23, 43, 45.
Ruth Price courtesy Weldon Trannies: page 24
Tony Rodd courtesy Weldon Trannies: pages 30-31.
Tony Ryan: pages, 6, 16, 18, 19, 20(above), 21, 25,46.
Weldon Trannies: front cover, opposite title page,
pages 10-11, 12, 29, 32, 35, 36, 37, 38 (above), 39, 41, 42 (right).

Published by Harlaxton Publishing Ltd
2 Avenue Road, Grantham, Lincolnshire, NG31 6TA, United Kingdom.
A Member of the Weldon International Group of Companies.

First published in 1990 (Limp)
Reprint 1991 (Cased)
Reprint 1992 (Cased)
Reprinted 1993

© Copyright Harlaxton Publishing Ltd
© Copyright design Harlaxton Publishing Ltd

Publishing Manager: Robin Burgess
Illustrations: Kathie Baxter Smith
Typeset in UK by Seller's, Grantham
Produced in Singapore by Imago

British Library Cataloguing-in-Publication data.
A catalogue record for this book is available from the British Library.
Title: Gardening with the Experts: Pruning.
ISBN:1 85837 026 4

CONTENTS

BASIC TECHNIQUES

To use this book successfully, it is essential to read this section first.

Not all plants need regular pruning. It depends on their style of growth. However, all plants, shrubs and trees should be groomed to remove dead or broken parts.

GROWTH PATTERNS
All flowering plants are built to the same basic plan. Shoots that consist of a series of joints (nodes) are separated by unjointed internodes. Initially nodes usually bear a leaf or leaves. Buds (embryo shoots) occur at the shoot tip and in each leaf axial.

Once leaves have fallen they are not replaced and stems may become bare, but in many plants the buds left behind grow into new leafy shoots. However, the stems of some evergreens (for example, most *Proteaceae* and conifers) have live auxiliary buds only where there are still leaves and cutting back to leafless wood causes the

*The flowering branch of a pear tree (**Pyrus communis**).*

death of the cut shoot.

In many shrubs a single trunk arises from the roots, while others have a suckering habit producing a thicket of stems. As new growth develops old stems die, so that clumps become choked with dead growth.

Flowers usually develop on young growth. Shoots of non-woody perennials commonly die after producing seeds to be replaced by others from buds at the base.

In many woody plants flowers grow on side shoots whose buds then shoot and flower in turn. Growth becomes crowded and feeble.

In a few families, as well as the buds that develop in leaf axials, each year at the end of the growing season a ring of buds forms just below the tip of each shoot. When growth begins again side shoots form from these buds only, so that the branches are arranged in whorls. Eventually these side shoots also develop whorls of branches. On plants with whorled growth, leaf axial buds do not normally give rise to shoots, but they may be induced to grow if the stem is damaged or pruned.

In families with whorled branches, the growth after flowering follows one of two distinct patterns. One type can be seen in members of the *Myrtaceae* family with bottlebrushlike inflorescences, such as *Callistemon* and *Beaufortia*, which produce their flowers not on side shoots but directly on the main stem. Each stem continues to grow beyond the flowers and may produce its next whorl of branches just above the inflorescence. The site of the old inflorescence may be marked by a bare section of stem, but in some species woody seed cases remain clinging to the stem.

Avoid cutting back into leafless wood when pruning conifers.

Another type of growth is common to rhododendrons and proteas in particular. At the end of the growing season of these plants a flower bud forms at the tip of the shoot, with a ring of growth buds below it. The shoots that have formed inflorescences do not grow any further, but once flowering is over the vegetative buds beneath the flower head develop into a whorl of new branches. As this pattern is repeated at every flowering, the stems become widely spread out. Some varieties do not flower for several years after planting. If no flower bud occurs at the shoot tip, a vegetative bud develops instead. In spring this bud grows into an extension of the main shoot, but side shoot development does not occur. Thus plants that do not flower tend to develop long, lanky, bare stems. In almost

all rhododendrons and some proteas live buds remain even on old wood, cutting back will activate them, so that severe pruning is a recognised method of rejuvenating old, straggly bushes.

A few shrubs and trees flower on spurs. These are specialised, much-compressed side shoots, sometimes branched, which live for many years, growing very little but bearing flowers annually. Spurs take time to establish, so the tip wood rarely bears flowers.

Most shrubs and trees have one annual growth period that is straight after flowering and then form new terminal buds. The new wood hardens progressively, until by winter, it is firm enough to snap and has a distinct bark.

It is usually distinguished from older

In most plants, flowers develop on new growth.

8

The junction between growth periods is marked on these trees by ring-shaped scars.
Pages overleaf: All plants should be groomed regularly.

Pruning a tree.

PURPOSEFUL PRUNING

Many young plants are pruned to stimulate branching as well as achieve more compact growth. Not all branch freely, so long bare stems may develop.

Auxiliary buds may fail to shoot because they are suppressed by hormones from the terminal bud. When the terminal bud is pruned off this effect vanishes and several shoots may develop. Usually the top bud becomes dominant and forms a new leader. Buds further down are usually influenced by the new tip to grow out sideways, but the one immediately below the top shoot may challenge it for dominance, forming an undesirable double head. Remove this second shoot or prevent the problem ever developing by destroying its bud at the first pruning. In many trees buds grow in a spiral around the stem and shoot development can be directed according to which are stimulated to grow.

Influence of a terminal bud on any shoot in the formation of laterals is diminished if the shoot is bent until nearly horizontal. This encourages, the development of

wood by a different colour, smoothness and lack of branching. Sometimes the junction between the new and old wood is marked by ring-shaped scars. In plants with only main shoots each whorl of branches is a record that represents one season's growth.

DEFINITIONS

Hard pruning: Removing half or more of the season's growth.

Light pruning: Removing one-third or less of the season's growth.

Pinching or stopping: Nipping the soft tips with the fingers.

Stubbing or stubbing back: Cutting a shoot to within two or three buds of its base.

Water shoot: A strong sucker on the main framework of a single-stem woody plant.

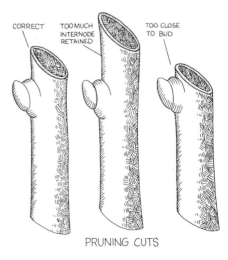

CORRECT   TOO MUCH INTERNODE RETAINED   TOO CLOSE TO BUD

PRUNING CUTS

flowers along the stems of climbing roses.

Actual result of pruning a shoot depends on the cut. If it is made on a length of stem with dormant buds it is likely several will form shoots. Usually the harder the cut, the more vigorous the subsequent growth. This technique is used to thicken hedges. Cuts should be made just far enough from nodes to avoid damaging them. Lengths of internode have no leaves to draw sap and soon die, leaving an unsightly snag that sometimes leads to extensive dieback.

Pruning may curtail growth. Where the node nearest the cut already bears a side shoot, buds further back are not usually activated and the shoot takes over as the head of the stem or branch. This allows leading shoots and laterals to be shortened without obvious mutilation or stimulating

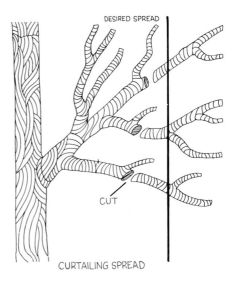

DESIRED SPREAD

CUT

CURTAILING SPREAD

unwanted shoots.

Having to prune a tree or shrub down to size is usually a sign of poor planning, although some are trained deliberately for special effects or to fit awkward spaces. All plants grow both sideways and upwards, which must be allowed for when planting. The worst problems seem to occur beside walkways and overhead wires.

MAJOR SURGERY

Sometimes it is necessary to amputate large tree limbs, which should not be attempted by amateurs unless the limb can be reached comfortably from the ground, or from a secure ladder. For safety, branches that are high enough to require climbing or special equipment should always be dealt with by a qualified arboriculturist, who can advise on health problems that may also make old trees unsafe.

It is essential to make the cut correctly if proper healing is to take place. Snags and torn bark both lead to rot and, apart from

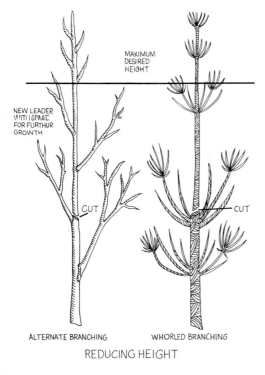

MAXIMUM DESIRED HEIGHT

NEW LEADER WITH DAMAGE FOR FURTHER GROWTH

CUT

CUT

ALTERNATE BRANCHING   WHORLED BRANCHING

REDUCING HEIGHT

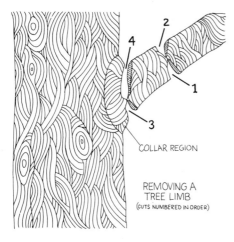

COLLAR REGION

REMOVING A
TREE LIMB
(CUTS NUMBERED IN ORDER)

TOOLS

Only prune with the correct and properly maintained tool. Not only is it inconvenient to struggle with substandard equipment, but tears and bruises of plant tissues prevent healing and make plants vulnerable to disease.

Secateurs should only be used for small stems, up to 15 mm in diameter. Most of these work well, but the lighter types are meant for picking flowers.

Stems in the range of 15 to 25 mm can be cut with long-handled loppers. Handle strength is important; light aluminium, for instance, often bends out of shape.

being unsightly, can eventually make trees dangerous. At the base of every branch is a slightly swollen region known as the collar. It has been found that if this is left intact the tree is able to resist rotting and usually the bark eventually heals over so that the wound is no longer visible. A collar occurs even on small branches, so when removing any branch, care should always be taken to retain them.

If bark is to heal over successfully it must form a smooth ring round the wound. This can be achieved with two saw cuts. The first quite shallow beneath the branch, and a second from above down to meet it. This will prevent a tear at the base of the wound which is otherwise unavoidable if branches of any size are removed with a single cut. A big limb should be reduced to a half-metre stub before the final operation. For extra support, tie it to the branch above.

Smooth the cut bark with a sharp knife to promote healing. Wound protection is no longer recommended, except for species susceptible to silverleaf fungus, when a fungicidal pruning paste should be used. (example: Prunus species and *silver birches*).

A weeping cherry.
Prunus are susceptible to silverleaf fungus.

Secateurs are used for the thinnest stems.

The basic pruning tools.

Always keep these tools clean and sharp. Blades will be coated with plant juices, so after use they should be rubbed with fine steel wool, then lightly oiled.

A professional sharpening service may be available at larger garden centres, although this is not difficult to do at home with an oilstone or a butcher's steel. Set blades as close as possible but short of binding.

A pruning saw is ideal for cutting small branches but becomes hard work on live wood that is much thicker than 100 mm, when a bowsaw or chainsaw works better. The most effective design is slightly curved and cuts on the pull stroke. Pruning saws have specially designed teeth for cutting live wood so a carpenter's saw is not a good substitute. Because of their shape, pruning saws can only be hand sharpened but they will stay sharp for many years with normal home use, especially if they are cleaned and oiled regularly.

ORNAMENTAL SHRUBS

LIGHT PRUNING GROUP

Plants in this group normally grow well and flower with a minimum of interference, but sometimes age or adverse circumstance can cause poor growth or dieback. For some of these species nothing can be done other than to replace them, while others may be revived by a single drastic pruning.

Much will depend on the immediate climatic conditions relating to the region and the specific variety under cultivation, if in any doubt consult your local nursery.

Single Stem with Lateral Shoots

These shrubs can go many years with just grooming (including deadheading), some thinning of weaker shoots and trimming to maintain good natural shape. For a denser growth pinch out tips in summer. Watch shrubs with variegated foliage for reversion, removing green shoots at source (but not green young shoots on purple *pittosporums*). *Photinias* need frequent light trimmings to stimulate coloured young growth. Remove stock shoots from grafted subjects.

A cottage with well-groomed ornamental shrubs.

Photinia '*Red Robin*'
should be clipped frequently.

Magnolia denudata
needs a minimum of pruning.

Leucadendron laurifolium, *a member of the* **Proteaceae** *family.*
Remove the lowest branches to make the plant more compact, but never cut into leafless growth.

*Protea cynaroïdes is an anomalous type of **Proteaceae**, with live buds right to its base.*

Many shrubs that are gaunt and spindly due to age or unfavourable environment, can be cut back hard (*Camellias* even to the ground) and will then sprout vigorously if helped by improved growing conditions.

Do not cut *Acacia* to leafless wood. (This treatment is not suitable for *Magnolias*, *Maples* or *Conifers* except *Yews*.)

This group includes: *Acacia*, *Arbutus*, *Aucuba*, box, broadleaf, *Camellia*, *Choisya*, conifers, *Coprosma*, *Corokia*, *Daphne*, *Euonymus* (evergreen kinds), *Garrya*, *Gaultheria*, holly, lilac, *Lophomyrtus*, *Magnolia*, *Maple*, *Photinia*, *Pieris*, *Pittosporum* and privet.

Single Stem with Branches Dividing after Flowering

Groom and deadhead these shrubs after flowering and make sprawling plants more compact by pruning their outer branches.

For members of the *Proteaceae* family, cut spent flowers just below the flower head, or include the stalk to make growth more compact. A few *proteas* have live buds on the bare wood, which allows them to be cut back hard if they become straggly. The buds are usually prominent structures that may spontaneously produce new shoots from the base of old stems. For example, of the species commonly grown, live buds occur on the bare wood of *Protea cynaroïde* (king protea) and *Protea grandiceps* (peach protea), but are absent from *Protea nerifolia*.

Deadhead *rhododendrons* by snapping off inflorescence just below the head, avoiding damage to the buds. Many old plants will become straggly and can be cut back hard, even into leafless wood. Dormant buds are hidden by bark, so expect to trim off some

Rhododendron *'Winsome'. Snap off the spent flower heads.*

*Unproductive **Azalea** stems should be shortened or cut off at ground level.*

stubs later. Shorten or cut to the ground unproductive stems of *Azaleas*.

In warm regions if you have *Callistemon* or *Beaufortia* take care to prune to a whorl of branches, never to leafless wood. Untidy growers benefit from thinning.

Multiple Stems
Fatsia, Leucothoë, Mahonias, Nandinas and *Pseudopanax* eventually become leggy, and shoots may be cut back to the ground to stimulate new growth.

REGULAR DETAILED PRUNING
In all except the cooler regions where frost will determine plant survival, in most cases prune as soon as blooms fade, including those giving several flushes like *Fuchsias*, catmint and roses.

Likewise, in spring prune all berried shrubs and half-hardy species like *Hibiscus* and *Lantana* if the climate permits growing on. Roses should be given a light pruning in late autumn before the ravages of frost and wind, with a heavier pruning in spring. Milder regions suited to many of the South African *Ericas* which flower most of the year, should be pruned or picked regularly, cut stems above a strong whorl of branches.

Flowering on Current Season's Growth
Because they need to grow before flowering, these shrubs seldom bloom until midsummer. If left unpruned they become leggy or crowded and prone to disease.

Prune deciduous varieties while dormant, but leave evergreens and half-hardy species until spring. Very vigorous varieties may be cut almost to the ground, leaving only two or three buds at the base of each stem, but for less vigorous species, or if a larger shrub is preferred, leave more length and in future seasons stub (cut back) shoots to two

or three buds from this framework. After the first year thin shoots out each season and stub back only the strongest.

Some shrubs do better if allowed to develop permanent leaders, which are only lightly tipped each year and whose side branches are stubbed back. Thin leaders out annually, replacing some with new shoots. Shrubs in this group include:
Abutilon: Train permanent leaders or for a smaller bush stub to a framework in spring.
Buddleia (not *alternifolia* or *globosa*): Stub to the base or a framework in spring.

*To rejuvenate plants of the **Pseudopanax** species, cut out the old stems.*

*Pages overleaf: **Wistaria** shrubs can be trained as standards.*

Caryopteris: Stub to the base in spring.
Ceanothus: Cut deciduous varieties to within 3" of old wood in spring, but stub evergreens to leaders.
Ceratostigma: Stub old or damaged shoots to the base in spring.
Escallonia: Trim only lightly to encourage flowering, remove flowered growth when complete. Cut established hedging hard.
Fuchsia: Hardy and hybrids can be stubbed to the base late autumn or spring. Remove dead or diseased wood in spring.
Hibiscus (hardy and tropical)*:* Stub back laterals to within 3" of old wood in spring. Long shoots may be shortened immediately after flowering..
Lantana: If plants are grown on prune main shoots back to 4" in early spring.

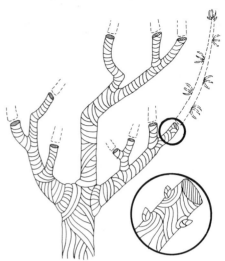

SHRUB FLOWERING ON NEW GROWTH STUBBED TO A FRAMEWORK

The vigorous growth of **Hibiscus** *can be controlled by spring pruning.*

Lavendula: Remove dead flower stems and lightly trim late summer. Straggly plants can be cut hard back in spring to promote bushy growth.
Lippia (Lemon verbena)*:* If frost damaged new growth will usually appear from base. Stub to a framework 12" above ground in spring.
Hydrangea: Remove dead heads after flowering or in spring. Stub back 2-3 year old shoots to the ground or a framework.
Potentilla: Keep bushy and vigorous by ground level removal of weak or old stems.
Beloperone (Shrimp plant-tropical)*:* Cut main stems back to half to maintain shape in early spring.
Spartium (Spanish broom)*:* Remove dead flower heads to prevent seeding, light trim in autumn encourages flowering.
Spiraea (x *bumalda, japonica*)*:* Stub to within 3-4" of base in spring.
Tamarix (summer-flowering *pentandra*)*:* Remove half to two thirds of previous seasons growth.

Lantana 'Golconda' *should be stubbed to 4" in spring.*

Rosa (Roses) belong in this group. Though commonly restricted by being grafted, they are true thickets and stems regularly die but are replaced.

Hybrid teas and floribundas: Prune bushes hard at planting. Remove weak or straggly growth (shoots less than pencil thickness). Cut flush with basal tissue, leaving no stub.

At least three strong stems will remain arranged evenly around the bush (two will do at a pinch). To get strong growth from as low as possible, cut stems hard, leaving no more than four or five buds that have either outward- or sideways-facing buds at the end. Hard prune the first year, but only repeat a second time on any plant which has not responded with strong growth. Replace if still spindly by the third winter.

When pruning established bushes, always remove all weak and dead shoots, leaving mainly smooth young stems. These arise from the base or from older wood, are dark green or purplish, usually have no branches or have strong shoots near the tips only. Old wood, generally much lighter, has a lot of weak branches on its lower part; retain it only if bearing young shoots further up.

In sheltered gardens allow tall growth, shortening unbranched shoots by about a third. If there are strong laterals around the tip, reduce these to two and then shorten each by about half. Some cultivars build up a permanent framework of wood with a light brown bark and new shoots grow from this (*floribundas*, some *hybrid teas*), allowing an impressive shrub to develop. On windy sites halving growth is safer.

Modern perpetual-flowering roses: need pruning after every flush of flowers. Do not snap off spent flowers, but cut back each stem sufficiently to stimulate strong new growth. The stalk immediately below the flower is normally rather thin and produces leaves with only three leaflets. Lower down the stem becomes much stouter and leaves bear five leaflets. Always make your cut close to one of these more vigorous leaves, choose a bud that points outside, away from the bush centre. While pruning, watch for dead or broken shoots and very spindly growth. If this unthrifty growth is removed regularly during the growing season, winter pruning will be simpler .

Standard roses: These are rose bushes on tall stems. Prune them a little harder when mature to avoid heavy flower heads which may damage stems.

Miniature roses (*including* **Patio roses**)**:** This category comprises a great variety of small roses, some only a few centimetres tall but all under 60 cm in height. Many are also available as standards. They should be pruned exactly as previously described for the larger rose bushes, using very sharp secateurs or even scissors to avoid bruising their delicate growth.

Shrub roses: Unlike the majority of *hybrid teas* and *floribundas*, all the roses in this group are pruned in such a way as to retain a permanent woody framework. These include a number of rose species as well as hybrids derived from them, some of which have been grown since antiquity. Many flower only once a year but have attractive fruits (hips).

Species roses: These can be left virtually unpruned most of the time, but eventually they become clogged with unproductive old wood and need thinning. They flower on growth developed the previous summer, any pruning should be done immediately after flowering, consider wind damage.

Page opposite: Mature standard roses should be pruned back a little harder than rose bushes.

Alba roses: Cut hard back some of the older wood each winter.

Gallica and Damask roses: Prune lightly in summer after flowering, removing dead wood and any shoots that look incapable of supporting flowers.

Centifolia and Moss roses: Reduce new shoots by at least one third each winter.

Rugosa roses: Remove old and weak wood each winter

'Bourbon' and 'Portland' roses: Most roses in this group flower more than once a year and should be deadheaded like hybrid teas. In winter reduce main shoots by one third and moderately prune the side shoots.

Hybrid musk roses: These are also repeat-flowering. The long, arching stems should be lightly tipped in winter, when old and weak growth should be cut out.

Modern shrub roses: These form vigorous, often spreading shrubs, some as tall as 2m, and flower repeatedly. They should be lightly pruned in winter, removing dead or very weak wood and shorten the remainder by about one third. The appearance and performance of those with large flowers is improved by deadheading after each flush of blooms.

Flowering on Previous Season's Growth
These shrubs mostly have a thicket habit, with stems flowering on the tip initially and thereafter on side shoots. After a first flowering cut stems back to a low, strong side shoot. For a year or two cut to shoots that are low on stems which have flowered, but remove some old stems to encourage new growth from the base.

Shrubs in this group include: *Buddleia (alternifolia, globosa)*: within 2-3" of old wood, *Deutzia* (tall kinds): remove old stems in late summer, *Currant* (flowering): cut back 1/3 in autumn, *Hypericum:*

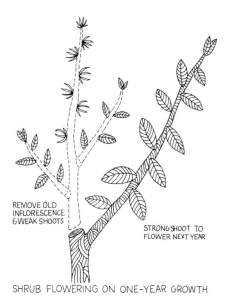

REMOVE OLD INFLORESCENCE & WEAK SHOOTS

STRONG SHOOT TO FLOWER NEXT YEAR

SHRUB FLOWERING ON ONE-YEAR GROWTH

within a few inches of the base each spring every few years, *Kerria*: cut to strong new growth after flowering, *Philadelphus*: thin out old wood take care of new growth for the following year, *Spirea (argutta)*: thin all species occasionally, and *Weigela*: remove 1-2 old stems after flowering, cut stems back to the base.

On non-thicket types prune away flower heads and any weak or worn-out growth. Shrubs in this category include: *Cytisus* (broom): after flowering up to 2/3 growth, *Cistus*: thin out damage only, *Hebe* (not whipcords): hard back in spring if leggy for new shoots from base, *Tamarix (tetrandra)*: after flowering.

Some needing special treatment are: *Berberis*: Prune deciduous in early spring, evergreens after flowering.

Heath and European heather: Shear heads immediately after flowering, remove most of the current season's growth.

Hydrangea macrophylla: Thin out at ground

level 2-3 year old stems to encourage new shoots in spring.

Luculia: Reduce to 3" as flowers fade.

Flowering on Spurs

Included in this group are:

Chaenomeles japonica: Produces an unmanageable tangle if untrained. On new plants select several well-balanced leaders, then remove surplus shoots. Trim side shoots to 3 or 4 buds to encourage spur formation. After flowering is established they require only light trimming, thinning and shaping.

Forsythia: A thicket; the first year shoots are vegetative only, producing flowering spurs in the second. Remove old damaged wood after flowering, on laterals cut back to 1-2 buds on the old wood.

Pruning for Foliage

In some deciduous shrubs vigorous young foliage is most spectacular, especially in the *Cotinus* (smoke tree): cut straggly growth shortened or removed in late winter.

Euonymus (spindle tree): shoots may be thinned out and shortened in late winter.

Paulownia imperialis (empress tree): cut to the soil level each spring if grown as a pot plant, becomes an accent shrub with huge, velvety leaves.

Evergreens improved by cutting back hard in spring and include *Teucrium fruticans*: and *Santolina* (cotton lavender): remove frosted tips in spring and shorten growth by half to limit spread.

Thymes: Clip most herbs several times a year for good, healthy production.

*Above: Herbs such as **tansy** should be cut back several times a year.*
*Pages overleaf: **Boronia mollis** should be reduced by half after flowering.*

FRUIT TREES

PIP FRUITS

These trees are spur-bearers pruned mainly in winter during frost free weather.

Apples and Pears

These trees do not fruit until sufficiently mature. Some take up to twenty years, but grafting on suitable stocks reduces the time to about two to three years for apples, a little longer for pears. As young trees find it hard to grow and crop, limit production until they have developed a sturdy framework. Initially some varieties will only crop every second year.

There are very large trees established on older properties, but new stock is now sold for home gardens on dwarfing stock. Apples eventually reach about two metres and pears between three and four, though they can be kept smaller.

Some trees are sold as single stems (whips) that can be trained as single-stem trees, or pruned to a vase shape of several leaders, while already branched ones are suitable only for multiple-stem growing.

Apple trees trained into a vase shape.

While apples can be managed either way, most amateurs find it easiest to grow pears with several leaders.

Framework Development:
For a vase shape the first pruning depends on whether the tree is a whip or branched. Whips must be decapitated at a suitable height for branching and all the top buds left to grow. A year's growth will produce several branches, and three strong ones should be chosen. These should not make a narrow angle with the trunk, or they may split later. Cut back hard, at the tip leave buds that face sideways rather than straight out or in. Remove all other shoots. After one more year select from four to six even-sized shoots well spaced around the tree and remove all other upright growth.

One leader or several are treated the same from now on. The aim is to develop a series of side branches (fruiting arms) at regular intervals, that will support fruiting wood. Where there is a single leader these limbs emerge all around the main trunk, but with multiple leaders inward-turning branches are removed, letting light and air into the centre.

To develop side shoots, decapitate stems just above the height you require a branch. The top bud will become a new leader and the second bud should be destroyed. The next bud or buds will grow out to form limbs, which may be thinned if too close. Repeat annually this until the tree is high enough, then cut back the leader to a weak side branch. If this weak shoot is not pruned its growth will be minimal and the height may be held for several years.

Strong shoots sometimes develop further down the stem, taking over as substitute leaders. These should always be cut away, leaving only the weak tip shoot.

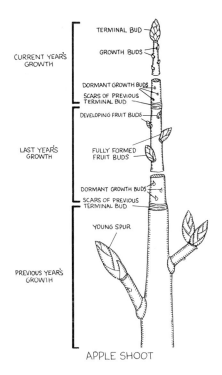

APPLE SHOOT

The fruiting arms ought to be lightly pruned each winter. If they grow fairly flat encourage this by cutting to an underside bud, but in some apples and most pears they have a strong urge to turn up. This can be combated by tying down for a few months or by pruning as shown. When they reach the required spread stop the growth at a weak side branch as described for leaders.

Any wood that remains for more than one year on an apple or pear tree carries vegetative buds which have not grown out into branches and may be transformed into fruit buds. In the first year of their development they are simple, torpedo-shaped structures protruding from branches much more prominently than vegetative buds. Each is capable of giving rise to a cluster of blossoms and ultimately, fruit. If the tip of the shoot has been cut, the bud nearest the cut end may also grow a new long shoot, but the majority of buds will develop into spurs. These are very compressed shoots that gradually evolve into branch struc-tures, with each branch ending in one or two fruit buds. Spurs are usually very long-lived. Those that form on the main trunk when the tree is first planted may continue to survive after the tree has reached full maturity.

As spurs become increasingly branched, the quality of fruit they produce falls off due to competition between the buds. Every two or three years the majority of buds should be pruned away, leaving only two or three of the strongest. Spurs on the main trunk or major branches of older trees

rarely produce good fruit as they suffer from poor sap supply and lack of light, so they should be removed completely.

It is possible to recognise unthrifty spurs during summer when the fruit is approach-ing maturity. Examine inner parts of the tree, looking for bunches of fruit that are smaller than normal, diseased or coloured poorly, then prune spurs flush to the stem.

The main crop on mature trees is borne on twigs springing from fruiting arms. These should be allowed to grow uncut for two years and should then be pruned back to where fruit buds have developed. If they are very long they should be shortened further, leaving only eight to ten buds. The end bud is likely to shoot during summer and at the next pruning this shoot should be shortened to one or two buds. This

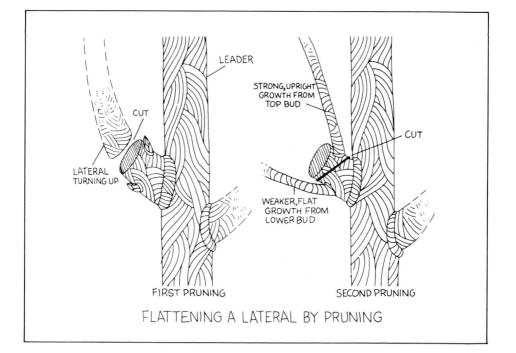

FIRST PRUNING

SECOND PRUNING

FLATTENING A LATERAL BY PRUNING

procedure will need to be repeated again at subsequent prunings.

On less vigorous trees, leave all fruiting shoots may result in a crop of undersized fruit. If this happens, prune completely about one third of the shoots, leaving the remainder evenly spaced. During the next summer check that enough wood has been removed.

After a few years some of the spurs may die, reducing the fruit crop. Cropping can often be improved by renewed pruning. At the base of each fruiting shoot are two or three tiny, dormant vegetative buds. If the rest of the shoot is removed, one or more of the buds will be stimulated to grow and new wood will be formed. During the next winter select the strongest new growth and remove the others.

A few apple trees (such as 'Rome Beauty' and 'Irish Peach') are tip bearers. Unpruned twigs develop fruit buds at the tips only, but if new laterals more than 10 cm long are cut back to about three buds, they will often be stimulated to develop fruit. Alternatively, strong laterals may be tied down so that their tips are lower than their bases, which will also stimulate extra fruit bud formation.

Established dwarf apple trees will usually need little pruning, but remove any twigs cluttering the inside of the tree as well as damaged, downward-turning or crossing wood. The quality of the crop will indicate whether any further pruning is necessary. If the fruit is good quality, no more pruning is needed, but undersized fruit implies that there are too many buds.

The fruiting arms of pear trees should be pruned lightly each winter.

Reduce their number by thinning the fruiting wood, remove ill-placed spurs and prune old, many-branched spurs.

So-called dwarf pear trees (grafted onto quince stocks) are much more vigorous than dwarf apples. Although they are easier to manage than full-sized trees, they do require similar pruning.

Quinces

These are not as vigorous as apple or pear trees. They are best grown as vase shaped trees with many leaders and no fruiting arms. Fruit grows only on new wood at the tips of the shoots, so cut back hard about a third of the shoots each year to encourage new growth, leave the remainder uncut to produce the crop. This method prevents the tree from becoming too tall.

STONE FRUITS

There is no effective way of dwarfing this group. The few genetic dwarfs produce inferior fruit.

Some of these trees produce strong water shoots from lower branches. Normally these should be completely removed, but in decrepit peaches they may be grown into a new tree, cutting the rest away.

Do major pruning in summer straight after fruiting to minimise the risk of deadly silverleaf disease.

Peaches and Nectarines

Trees in warm regions need little pruning, beyond the removal of any strong growth near the top, but in cold climates a lot of extra buds grow, necessitating thinning. Train on a single stem and each year

In cold regions, peach trees need thinning.

remove the strong early-season growth, leaving later-formed, weaker wood which fruits better.

Fruit develops only on pale reddish brown growth of the current year. Very heavy bearers should be winter-pruned as well, thinning out up to half the fruiting twigs and lightly shortening the remainder.

Plums

Both Japanese and European plums normally grow best in a vase shape.
European plums: Select leaders, cut out excess shoots, and leave unpruned for a year or two until established. Fruit is borne on long-lived spurs. Each summer shorten strong young shoots as necessary to control height and remove any dead, overcrowded or crossed laterals

Japanese plums: Willowy growth may need staking in the early years, or cutting to an inside bud to make it more upright, but leave upright growers unshorn initially, only cutting out excess leaders. Thereafter, prune off excessive upright growth and regularly cut out dead, crossing and very droopy wood, keeping the tree centre clear.

Cherries

Prune minimally once a framework is established. Some may need annual work to control size.

Apricots

Plump fruiting spurs form on one year-old wood and last three to four years. Remove unfruitful wood annually. Pruning laterals in summer encourages spur formation.

Cherry trees may need regular pruning to control their size.

Unfruitful wood should be removed annually from apricot trees.

In warm regions older wood should be removed from mature lemon trees.

CITRUS FRUITS

In warm regions, these grow naturally into well-shaped trees, but some produce unwanted water shoots on the stem, close to the main branches. Pruning can be done at any time except when frost is expected, but is most convenient after harvest.

Orange and Grapefruits

In warm regions, established orange and grapefruit trees need little pruning beyond removal of water shoots, dead or diseased wood, though 'Wheeny' grapefruit trees may be topped if they show a tendency to biennial bearing.

Lemons and Mandarines

In warm regions 'Eureka' lemons sometimes have spindly, naked branches, which should be shortened. Other dense bushy types, like 'Meyer' and mandarines such as 'Clementine' or 'Thorny', benefit from a moderate thinning of fruit-bearing wood.

Revive aging citrus trees by removing older wood. It is always best to thin out laterals along a branch, or shorten it to a lateral rather than a dormant bud, fruiting laterals are slow to develop from cut ends.

HEDGEROW FRUITS

Blackcurrants

Cut out wood that has fruited. Retain new, smooth, whitish growth, especially those coming from the base.

Redcurrants

Grow on a single stem with eight to twelve leaders. Stub back all laterals in winter to induce spur formation.

Gooseberries

Train as an open bush, removing crossing shoots and pruning out older wood each winter, when leaders should be cut back by half. In midsummer prune all new laterals to five leaves, then shortening in winter to two buds.

In warm regions, stablished orange trees need a minimum of pruning.

SUBTROPICAL FRUITS

Avocados

These trees need little pruning, although the spreading kinds may need to have some branches shortened, especially if they are long and drooping and likely to break with a heavy crop. For tall growers such as the 'Hass' variety, tips of the leaders can be pinched in the early years for a more manageable height. As trees mature, the inside branches always die off and should be removed.

Babacos and Mountain Pawpaws

These plants are closely related and are both usually grown as a single stem. Any side shoots that grow should be rubbed off as they appear until about spring, when one should be allowed to develop as a replacement for the old fruiting stem. This new shoot will start fruiting soon after the old stem is removed. If preferred, original stems may be retained for a second year.

Feijoas

At planting, these trees should be trimmed to a single stem, with lowest side branches 50 cm from the ground. In the first season tip back to 8 cm all shoots as they develop to encourage vigorous branching.

In subsequent years only light pruning is needed to maintain a good shape, but keep growth above the ground and thin out branches to allow light to penetrate into the interior of the bush. The fruit is borne at the base of the new season's growth.

Tamarillos

Pruning these trees is optional in a home garden, but seedling plants become very tall and straggly if they are not stopped when they are about 1 metre high. Plants grown from cuttings, in contrast, have a low, bushy habit and require removal of some of the lower branches for adequate ground clearance.

Tamarillos bear fruit on current season's growth, so apart from removing dead and damaged wood, sturdier trees and better crops will result if laterals that have fruited are shortened in spring to encourage strong new shoots. The earlier pruning is done, the earlier the crop will mature.

MISCELLANEOUS

PLANTS ON SUPPORTS
Soft Fruits
These have a floppy, thicket growth style.
Raspberries: either bunch and tie canes or grow them between wires or strings. After midsummer cut all canes that have fruited to the ground and tie new growth. Thin new canes in winter and tip lightly.
Blackberries: are usually grown on two or more parallel wires held by stout posts.

Remove canes that have fruited immediately after fruiting. Bunch and tie new summer growth.

Grapevines
Avoid spring pruning, since it will cause copious bleeding.

The vine is trained on two horizontal

Pruned shrubs, trees and standards in a manicured garden.

41

wires about 600 mm apart. Tie the young vine to a stake. Decapitate it in winter just above the lower wire. The top bud will grow into a new leader and the next two shoots that develop should be trained along the wire in opposite directions to form two fruiting rods. When the new leader reaches the second wire, it should be decapitated in turn and the two topmost shoots that develop trained as a second pair of rods.

Side shoots eventually bear fruit. During summer pinch fruiting shoots to two leaves beyond the bunch, and shorten all non-fruiting wood to 500 mm, repeating as necessary. In winter stub back all laterals to two buds. If a rod becomes unfruitful with age, choose a lateral as close to the main stem as possible and let this shoot grow unpruned all summer, tying it loosely to the old rod. In winter prune away the old growth and tie replacement rod to wires.

Kiwi Fruit

These vines are heavy and need strong supports. Train them on a 1.8 metre high wire fence, a T-bar or an overhead pergola. Each female vine should have a single trunk with two arms extending in opposite directions from its top. To supply sufficient pollen, only a small male vine is required and a single short arm should support enough side shoots.

Vines bear fruit on only the first three to

Blackberries can be trained on wires supported by posts.

Grapevines should not be pruned in spring.

six buds of the current season's growth and this must spring from a one-year-old branch. During summer the fruiting canes will continue to grow, but in addition strong new shoots will spring from the main stem. In mid-summer the shoots that have fruited should be cut out and smooth new shoots retained. If there are insufficient new shoots, some of the strongest shoots that have already fruited can be kept for another year. All the shoots kept will need tipping to remove weak, twisted end growth.

Passionfruit
Train four vigorous basal shoots into a fan shape on a permanent framework, tipping each to produce eight secondary leaders. Fruit is borne on the laterals of the current year. When these have fruited once, stub them back to two buds in late autumn, in the same way as for a grapevine. Cut out spindly and diseased shoots and train in a few new basal shoots to replace any unthrifty leaders.

Climbing Roses
A climbing rose is simply a bush that has extra-long canes needing support. This may be provided by three parallel wires either free-standing or across the face of a wall. Alternatively, individual ties may be fastened to the wall where needed.

The rose shoots should be arranged in a two-dimensional fan shape then tied in place. As they must be untied and rearranged each winter, winding shoots into a trellis or wire netting is inappropriate.

Replacement shoots will grow each summer. They are brittle and should be tied to prevent wind damage. Shoots growing at right angles to the support can not be trained in effectively and are best

cut out as soon as noticed.

In winter untie all the shoots and cut away old and weak canes, leaving no more than seven to form a new fan. If there are insufficient smooth, unflowered canes, the strongest older growths may be retained, stubbing all their laterals to two buds.

Wistaria
Either grow *Wistaria* freely over an old tree or train rods on a wall. Cut side shoots to about 200 mm long in summer, shorten in winter to four or five buds to form spurs. Cut surplus basal shoots during summer.

Espaliers
These are time consuming and only for the

Wistaria can be trained over a pergola.

leisurely. Espaliers are bushes and trees trained in two dimensions. They are used for decoration, as space-savers and to give tender shrubs wall protection.

Pip and stone fruit trees may be trained on free-standing wires or board fences, since your regional climate maybe too hot or dry to use brick or stone walls as usually recommended in traditional British sites.

Use up to five horizontal wires training either parallel side shoots like a grapevine (pip fruits only) or upright shoots in a fan or gridiron configuration. Retain only shoots parallel with the wall.

On pip fruits only young growth is supple enough to train, so tie in the shoots loosely as they grow. During summer cut out any unwanted strong shoots and shorten the

rest to 120 mm, cutting back to three buds in winter. Next season these should form fruit buds. On older trees renew unfruitful laterals by cutting back to basal buds.

Pyracanthas can be espaliered without supports, simply by pinching all forward pointing shoots.

Bougainvilleas enjoy a hot wall. Train a permanent framework, pinching out unwanted shoots in summer, and cut back side shoots to two buds in spring.

TREES

Remove with secateurs any stray shoots spoiling the outline or shear lightly. Many conifers look more attractive if bottom branches are retained. Shorten vertical growth by removing tiers of branches.

*Above: **Bougainvillea** trailing over a sunny wall.*
Page opposite: A climbing rose pruned to grow over a pergola.

Others

If trees must be tailored to fit a restricted area, curtail growth early enough to avoid major surgery. To form a standard, remove bottom branches progressively so as not to deprive young tree of too much nourish ment. Some trees are sold as standards that are ready-prepared.

If trees cast excessive shade, let more light in by thinning rather than mutilating with decapitation.

The wrong way to top Cypresses.

INDEX

The page numbers in **bold type** indicate illustrations .